CHILDREN'S
-Party-
THEMES

Devised and illustrated by

Clare Beaton

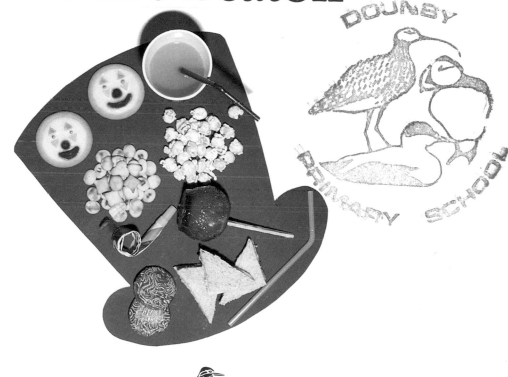

Kingfisher Books

CONTENTS

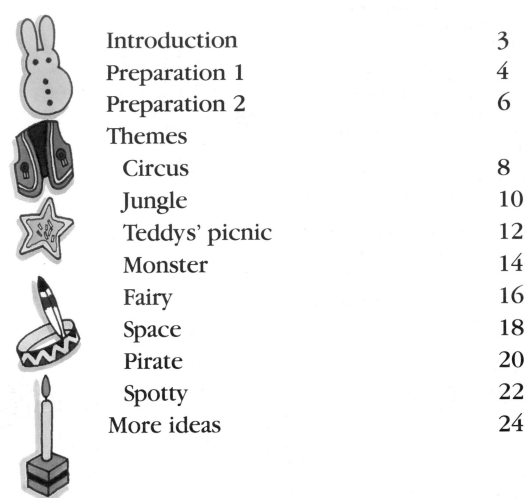

Produced by Times Four Publishing Ltd
Art and editorial direction: Tony Potter
Copy editor: Nicola Wright
Home Economist: Nicola Bereen

Kingfisher Books, Grisewood & Dempsey Ltd,
Elsley House, 24-30 Great Titchfield St, London W1P 7AD

First published in 1991 by Kingfisher Books

10 9 8 7 6 5 4 3 2 1

Colour separations by RCS Graphics, Leeds
Typeset by C-Type, Horley, Surrey
Printed in Spain

BRITISH LIBRARY CATALOGUING IN PUBLICATION DATA
Beaton, Clare
    Children's party themes.
    1. Entertainment. Parties. Children's
    I. Title   II. Series
    793.21

ISBN 0-86272-704-9

INTRODUCTION

Having a theme to a party greatly adds to the fun and excitement, and encourages children to join in and use their imaginations.

This book is full of ideas and useful tips to help make the party a success. Each section covers the sending of invitations, decoration, dressing up, food, games and suggestions for what to give as going home presents.

Remember to tailor the party to the children attending. Very young children do not enjoy games with complicated rules. In general, keep games simple and vary the pace with quiet games alternating with more boisterous activity. Parties involving different age groups and mixes of boys and girls need careful planning. However much you may wish otherwise, boys and girls may have different ideas about what they want to wear, eat and play.

However, a theme party needn't require extra work on your part, just some forward planning. For example, much of the food can be made in advance and then kept in the freezer or in airtight containers. Children love music, so choose some records or tapes for them to sing and dance to. Try and enlist some extra adult help on the day of the party to ensure everything goes smoothly.

Invitations

This book gives you ideas to help you make party invitations. Why not get the birthday child to help you. This will give you both a fun activity to share.

If you are going to use envelopes, remember to measure them first, so you can make the invitations to fit.

Give invitations out about two weeks before the day - early enough to avoid disappointment on refusal, but not so early that the date gets forgotten!

Make your invitations from brightly coloured paper or card. Keep illustrations simple and uncluttered. If you have access to a photocopying machine you can simply make copies of a drawing, stick them on to coloured paper and colour them in.

Collage is also fun, easy to do and very effective. Cut or tear up old magazines or comics and stick the pictures on to card. Differently sized lettering from old newspapers looks good rearranged to spell out the word 'party'.

On the inside or back of the invitation write the date, place, and starting and finishing times of the party. For small children's parties, an hour and a half is probably long enough. Three hours is a sensible limit for older children.

Please come to JACK'S PARTY on Tuesday 1st March at 26 Valley Road from 3:00pm - 4:00...

Dressing up

Keep dressing-up clothes simple and comfortable to wear. Improvise with what old clothes you may already have. Alternatively, jumble sales and charity shops are good places to find garments, for example old curtains for cloaks and wings. Make sure they are clean!

You could start a theme party by getting the children to make something to go with their outfits, or a prop for a game. This activity can help guests get over any initial shyness and provide something for them to do while waiting for everyone to arrive.

Have everything laid out on a table ready for the children. Have all masks, badges and hats cut out and ready to be decorated, to avoid children using scissors. Have a good selection of sticky shapes, sequins, feathers, glitter, glue and felt-tip pens set out. Badges are simple to make from circles of card with a safety pin taped to the back.

Decorations

Balloons and streamers always look great at any party. Put a couple of balloons on the front door to emphasize where the party is being held. If you're holding your party outdoors, hang a bunch of balloons from a tree or bench.

For a particularly decorative look, attach a thread or string to the ceiling or walls so that it hangs above the party tea table, then drape streamers over it. You can adapt this idea with your theme in mind, for example thin black plastic streamers and cut-out spiders look great at a monster party.

If you buy balloons, hang them in big bunches for maximum effect. You could then give one to each guest as they leave.

If you want to be more ambitious and reinforce your theme, you can stick cut-out paper shapes to the windows and doors. You could hang ragged black plastic bin liners from doorways at a monster party, tinsel for a fairy party, and green crêpe paper for a jungle party.

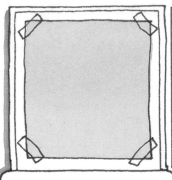

Coloured crêpe or tissue paper taped on to windows will give an unusual light and add to the atmosphere.

You might even get your guests to help with the decorating by colouring in a simple mural with felt-tip pens, outlined on lining paper (or the back of old wallpaper) pinned to a wall. You could start the party this way. It doesn't have to be finished - your own children will enjoy carrying on if you leave it up for a few days.

Continue the theme when decorating the table. For a jungle party you can cover plates or trays with green paper leaves, or use aluminium foil for a space party. Limiting the scheme to just one or two colours is most effective.

Games

Have a list of games and a box of props and small prizes (if you want to give any) all ready before the party. Be prepared for more games than you think you will need. Try not to have gaps between the games as the children will get restless. If the weather permits, hold the party outdoors where there is plenty of space. You could perhaps then have a barbecue party. However, it's always a good idea to have alternative indoor games planned, in case it rains or turns cold.

Adapt the games to fit your theme. For example, rather than have *Pin the tail on the donkey,* you could have *Pin the helmet on the spaceman* at a space party, or *Pin the star on the fairy's wand* at a fairy party.

Treasure hunts are always fun and can be written to a theme with an appropriate prize. Children enjoy hunting for small hidden objects so these could also be chosen with the theme in mind. Hide chocolate coins at a pirate's party and small plastic animals at a jungle party.

Food

Most party food will be the same whatever party you have. But try to include a few things that are in keeping with your theme. Whatever you do, keep it simple, easy to eat, but fun and attractive.

Biscuits and fairy cakes are easy to make using cutters and cake tins. You can make them well in advance to keep in the freezer.

Encourage your child to help you make the food, but discourage the use of too much dark or lurid food colouring as this will look, and be, less appetising.

If you're having a picnic, you can pack up individual boxes (taking extra supplies to top up). Buy the boxes from bakers or use old ice cream tubs.

Cake

The climax of the party is often the cake. Here you can spend a bit more time on a surprise cake to suit your theme. Using differently sized sponge cakes, Swiss rolls, wafers, fondant icing and so on, all sorts of shapes and effects can be achieved.

If everyone is too full to eat a piece of cake, give out slices, wrapped in paper napkins or tin foil, to take home.

Going Home

Even going home presents can be chosen with the theme in mind. There are endless cheap, small presents and sweets to choose from. If you like you can replace the usual plastic party bags with paper cones, small boxes and so on.

Assemble all the gifts well in advance and keep them together in a box or basket. For a personal touch you could stick on individual name labels.

CIRCUS

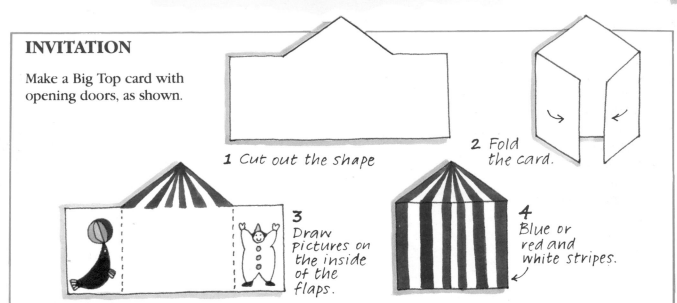

INVITATION

Make a Big Top card with opening doors, as shown.

1 Cut out the shape

2 Fold the card.

3 Draw pictures on the inside of the flaps.

4 Blue or red and white stripes.

DRESSING UP

Dress up as a clown, strong man, tightrope walker, acrobat, or ringmaster.

Clown
Mix small and large clothes

Stick on or sew bright patches

Acrobat
Leotard and tights with net frill.

Decorated yoghurt pot for hat.

Use face paints for greater effect

Strongman
Fur fabric suit and card weights

GAMES

- Make your own *Pin the nose on the clown's face.*
- See who can balance an object on their nose for the longest time. You could use a ball or a matchbox.
- Play *Ringmaster says* as a version of 'Simon says'. The ringmaster could wear a top hat.
- *Hoopla:* cut hoops out of cardboard and throw them over mini bags of sweets laid out on the floor.

Ball of red fondant icing for nose →

CAKE

Using a round sponge cake, decorate with a clown's face on top of fondant icing.

DECORATIONS

Hang up lots of brightly coloured balloons and streamers.

↑ *Cut star shapes out of fondant icing*

FOOD

Cut top hat place mats out of paper.

Serve:
- Popcorn.
- Toffee apples.
- Biscuits iced with clown faces, or in the shape of bow ties, 'spotted' with sweets.
- 'Red noses' made from cherry tomatoes or glacé cherries stuck on biscuits with cheese or icing.

GOING HOME

At the end of a circus party you could give out giant balloons, party blowers, dolly mixtures, red noses and bubble mixture. Buy or make simple party hats (from large yogurt pots) to put the presents in.

JUNGLE

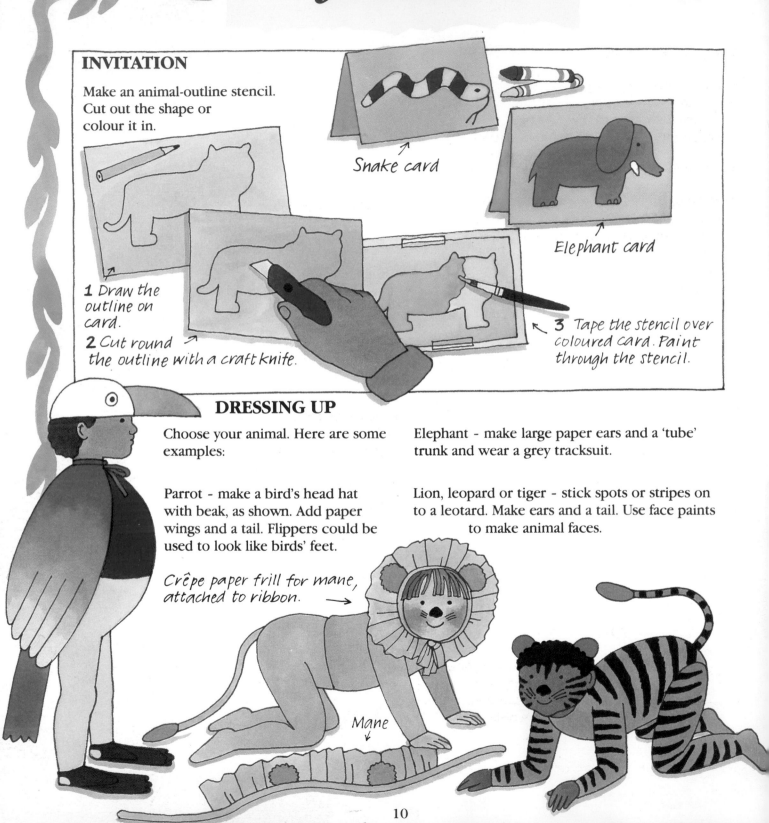

INVITATION

Make an animal-outline stencil. Cut out the shape or colour it in.

Snake card

Elephant card

1 Draw the outline on card.

2 Cut round the outline with a craft knife.

3 Tape the stencil over coloured card. Paint through the stencil.

DRESSING UP

Choose your animal. Here are some examples:

Parrot - make a bird's head hat with beak, as shown. Add paper wings and a tail. Flippers could be used to look like birds' feet.

Elephant - make large paper ears and a 'tube' trunk and wear a grey tracksuit.

Lion, leopard or tiger - stick spots or stripes on to a leotard. Make ears and a tail. Use face paints to make animal faces.

Crêpe paper frill for mane, attached to ribbon. →

Mane
↓

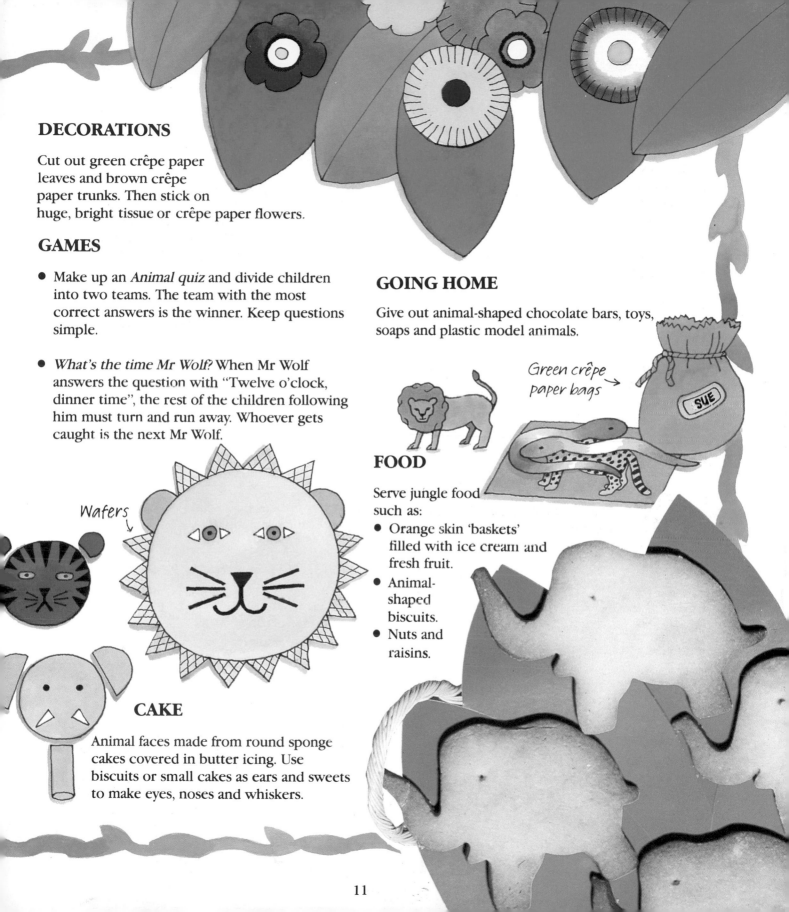

DECORATIONS

Cut out green crêpe paper
leaves and brown crêpe
paper trunks. Then stick on
huge, bright tissue or crêpe paper flowers.

GAMES

- Make up an *Animal quiz* and divide children
  into two teams. The team with the most
  correct answers is the winner. Keep questions
  simple.

- *What's the time Mr Wolf?* When Mr Wolf
  answers the question with "Twelve o'clock,
  dinner time", the rest of the children following
  him must turn and run away. Whoever gets
  caught is the next Mr Wolf.

Wafers

CAKE

Animal faces made from round sponge
cakes covered in butter icing. Use
biscuits or small cakes as ears and sweets
to make eyes, noses and whiskers.

GOING HOME

Give out animal-shaped chocolate bars, toys,
soaps and plastic model animals.

Green crêpe
paper bags

SUE

FOOD

Serve jungle food
such as:
- Orange skin 'baskets'
  filled with ice cream and
  fresh fruit.
- Animal-
  shaped
  biscuits.
- Nuts and
  raisins.

TEDDYS' PICNIC

INVITATION

Make a 'teddy' mask and use it as an invitation.

Trace this shape on to thin card and cut it out.

Write the party details on the back. Add a note asking guests to bring the mask, but have a few extra ready for those who forget.

Thread thin elastic through holes and knot.

DRESSING UP

Ask guests to wear their mask and bring their own teddy with them.

DECORATIONS

Tie balloons to a bench or tree by the picnic spot. Spread out a colourful tablecloth and rugs to sit on.

GAMES

- Get everyone to sing *Teddy bear's picnic*.
- Invent games using teddies, for example, who can throw teddy furthest! Give winning teddies new ribbons.
- Act out *Goldilocks and the three bears*.

FOOD

Try:
- Teddy-shaped biscuits.
- Honey and marmalade sandwiches.
- Honey cakes.
- Sugar buns.

GOING HOME

Buy tiny toy teddies, jelly teddies, or any item with teddy bears on it. There are many picture books featuring teddies of various kinds, as well as Paddington, Pooh Bear, Rupert Bear and other famous bear stories.

CAKE

Make a Teddy cake, using one small cake for the head, a larger one for the body, biscuits for ears and sponge fingers for the arms and legs. Cover with butter icing, positioning sweets for eyes and a nose.

Head

Ears

Legs

Body

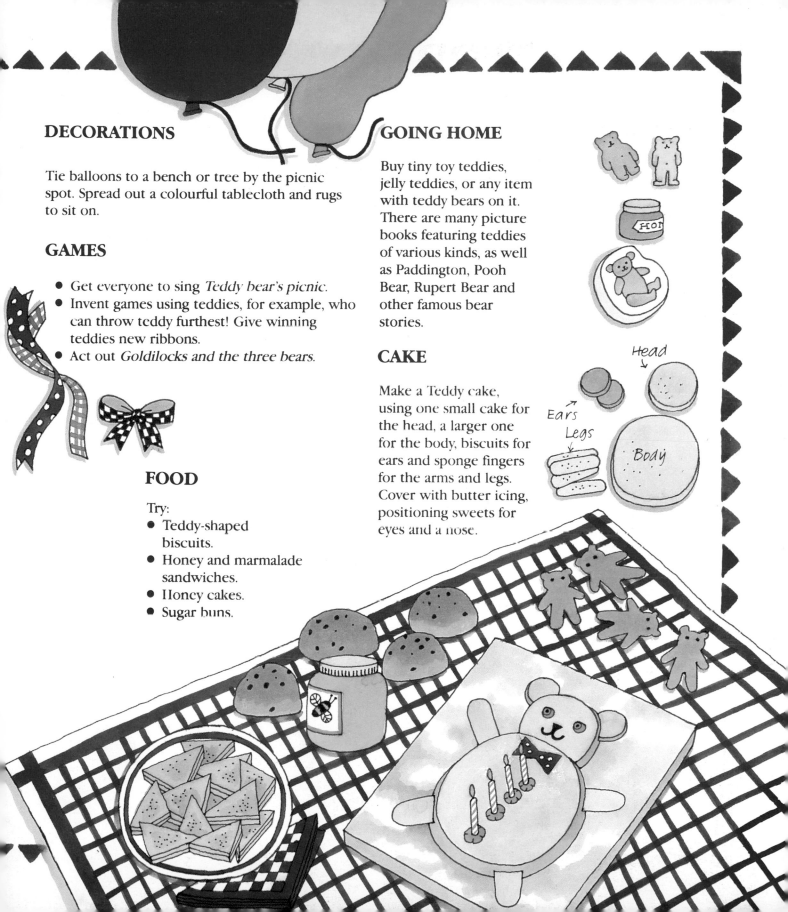

MONSTER

Fold in four

Cut

Paint or draw a monster.

INVITATION

A simple monster pop-up card coloured in lurid colours such as black, purple, lime green and orange looks very effective.

DRESSING UP

Wear black or purple and add any combination of tails, masks, antennae, horns, cloaks, false nails and teeth. Good materials to use include shiny plastic, net and fur. Making up faces with face paints can add the finishing touch.

'Creepy crawlies' on pipe cleaners fixed to head bands.

Flippers

Black bin liner cloak

Make card mask and add wool hair.

Cardboard mask with elastic

Paper Devil's tail

Black stocking mask with paper decorations.

CAKE

To make a monster cake, place a small pudding basin sponge cake on top of a round sponge cake, and then cover the shape with green runny glacé icing. Use liquorice for hands and mouth, and large sweets for eyes.

FOOD

Serve:
● Sugar 'rats'. ● Purple jelly. ● Small 'spider' sponge cakes or doughnuts with liquorice 'legs'.
● Black and green grapes.

Mashed up black jelly

GAMES

● Blindfold children so that they have to guess by smell and feel what certain unusually textured objects are, for example, cooked spaghetti.

● Let them search with their hands for small objects hidden in mashed up jelly. These games could be messy, so provide aprons and waterproof table covers.

DECORATIONS

Cut black bin liners and crêpe paper into tatters to hang around the room. Cover the windows in tissue paper with shapes cut out. You could make spiders' webs out of black wool. Hang cut-out or plastic spiders from thread strung above the table.

GOING HOME

Give out monster sweets and black balloons. Joke blood is always popular, as are plastic flies and spiders. You could also make simple 'finger' monster puppets.

Tied up black plastic or paper

FAIRY

INVITATION

Cut stars out of silver and gold paper. Then stick glitter on one side and write the party details on the other.

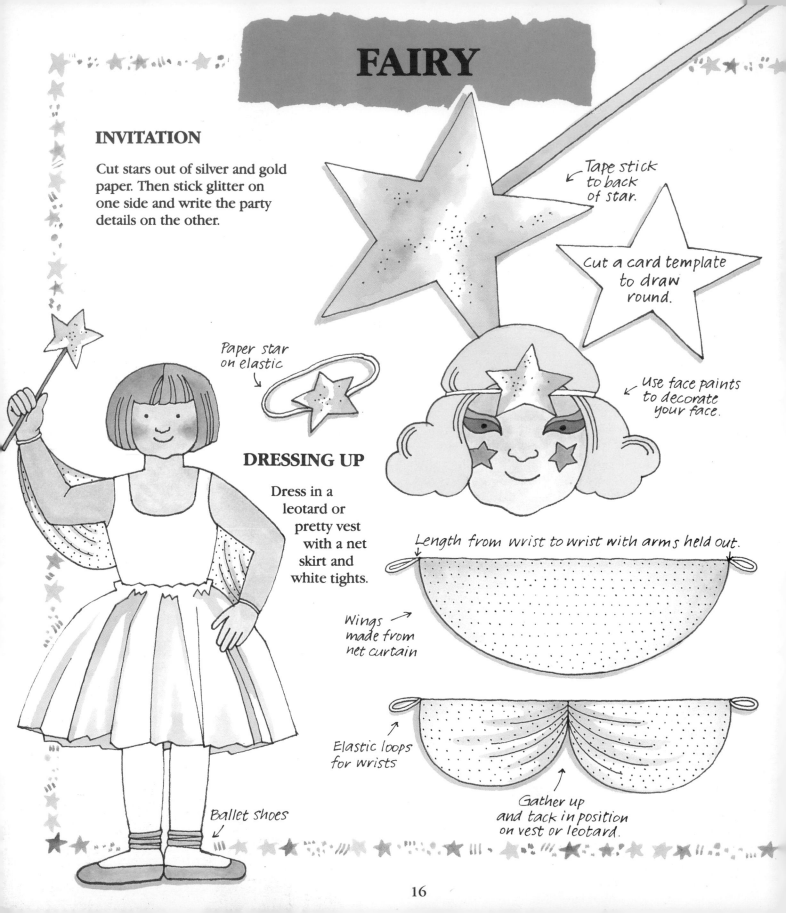

Tape stick to back of star.

Cut a card template to draw round.

Paper star on elastic

Use face paints to decorate your face.

DRESSING UP

Dress in a leotard or pretty vest with a net skirt and white tights.

Length from wrist to wrist with arms held out.

Wings made from net curtain

Elastic loops for wrists

Gather up and tack in position on vest or leotard.

Ballet shoes

DECORATIONS

Hang tinsel above the table over a string.

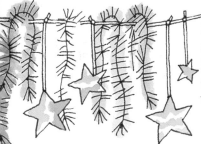

Hang silver and gold stars and moons from the ceiling on threads, or stick them to windows and doors.

GAMES

- Dancing to music.

- *Pin the star on the fairy's wand.*

- You could hire a magician to do a magic show.

FOOD

Make or buy:
- Tiny iced biscuits.
- Star-shaped decorated biscuits.
- Fairy cakes
- Pastel-coloured meringues stuck together with cream.

CAKE

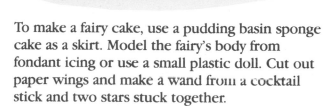

To make a fairy cake, use a pudding basin sponge cake as a skirt. Model the fairy's body from fondant icing or use a small plastic doll. Cut out paper wings and make a wand from a cocktail stick and two stars stuck together.

GOING HOME

You could make pretty cones out of paper doilies and fill them with sweets wrapped in shiny metallic paper, tiny biscuits and tubes of glitter.

SPACE

INVITATION

Cut out rocket or planet shapes from card.

Come to JOE'S Party

Emma's Space Party at 15 The Glade

20th March from 2.00pm - 3.00pm

Colour the shapes in and write the party details on with a silver pen. Then stick on silver and gold stars.

DRESSING UP

Dress in all-in-ones, boiler suits or track suits, adding belts. Stick on badges and wear a helmet which you could make using a hat or crash helmet decorated with stars and symbols.

Laser gun made from a plastic bottle, cardboard tube and plastic tub.

Wellington boots

GAMES

- Play *Pass the space parcel*, wrapping the prize in layers of silver paper.

- Hold a competition to see who can draw the best Alien.

CAKE

Paper flag on cocktail stick.

Lego models

Make a 'moon cake' using a pudding basin sponge cake covered with fondant icing. Make jagged holes in the icing for craters. For the finishing touch, stick on toy space men and space buggies.

GOING HOME

There are lots of space theme sweets you could give out, including Mars bars, Milky Ways, Space Dust and Flying Saucers. Or you could give toy rockets, sticky stars, or books about space.

DECORATIONS

Hang up silver foil moons and stars. Buy silver balloons or you could spray ordinary ones with silver spray paint.

FOOD

- Serve individual 'space meals', packed picnic style in named boxes. Include items such as moon rock cakes, and sandwiches wrapped in foil.

Joe

Cake box or ice cream tub

Plastic containers of drink

19

PIRATE

INVITATION

X marks the spot for this party. Cut out an island shape from thick paper and colour one side. Then write the party details on the back. Alternatively, glue or draw a white skull and crossbones on black card.

DRESSING UP

Make pirate pants from old trousers with jagged cut-off legs and patches sewn on. Add stripey T-shirts and spotty handkerchiefs. Or you could make a paper pirate's hat with skull and crossbones.

For the character Long John Silver, hop on one leg and use a wooden stick as a crutch. You could even put a toy parrot on your shoulder.

Hoop earrings sewn to scarf.

Black card eye patch on elastic

Wellington boots or bare feet depending on weather

DECORATIONS

Cut out paper palm trees and add green paper leaves and cut-out or use toy parrots.

GAMES

- Make up a *Treasure hunt* around the house or garden to find hidden chocolate coins.
- Invent a simple secret code, using it to write clues to the whereabouts of 'buried' treasure.

GOING HOME

Chocolate money, small plastic ships, eye patches, sweet necklaces, bracelets and plastic jewellery could make up pirate's treasure. As a novelty, cut up spotty cotton material into squares and tie on to a stick for them to carry it home in.

FOOD

You could serve:
- Boats made from halved bread rolls covered with cream cheese, or peanut butter, with paper sails on cocktail sticks.
- Biscuits iced with skull and crossbones, or wrapped in coloured foil paper to look like jewels.

CAKE

Cut a loaf-shaped sponge cake into a prow at one end. Use brown fondant icing to cover the sides and top. Add sails and flags, using sweets for portholes.

Make sails and flags out of thick paper.

Knitting needles or wooden skewers for masts.

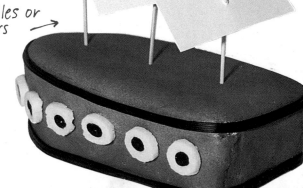

SPOTTY

INVITATION

Decorate a thick paper or card circle with coloured spots. You could write the party details round in a circle, too.

Lightly draw guidelines with a pair of compasses to help write your message in a circle.

DRESSING UP

Wear spotty clothes, or paint lots of spots on old plain clothes with fabric pens.

Stick adhesive paper circles on to fabric →

Alternatives

Or you could have a stripey party or a party with one particular colour, and dress in appropriate clothes.

DECORATIONS

Stick or draw spots on to the tablecloth, walls, paper cups etc. . Thread large paper circles on to ribbons and hang them up as decorations. Or have one colour for everything if you are having a one-colour party.

GOING HOME

Anything circular or spotted would be suitable, for example, Smarties, marbles, dice-shaped erasers and sheets of sticky paper spots.

GAMES

- Hold tiddlywink races, making a circular board with a centre target marked on it. The first child to flick a tiddlywink on to the target is the winner.
- Move tiddlywinks from one bowl to another by sucking them up with a straw. The child who moves the most in a given time is the winner.
- Organize a Smarties hunt.

Plastic counters

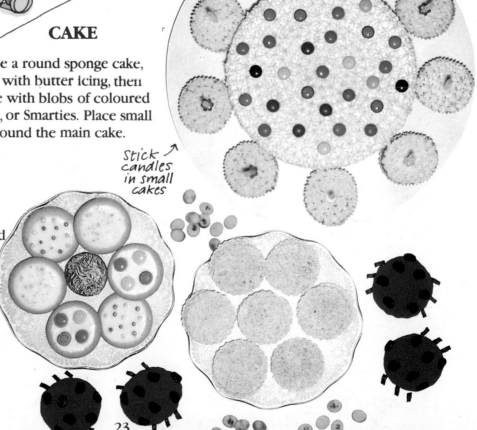

CAKE

Use a round sponge cake, cover with butter icing, then decorate with blobs of coloured glacé icing, or Smarties. Place small fairy cakes around the main cake.

Stick candles in small cakes

FOOD

Serve:
- Round biscuits decorated with round sweets.

- Sandwiches cut into circles with biscuit cutters.

23

MORE IDEAS

Christmas Party

Cut out Christmas tree-shaped invitations from green paper and stick on coloured spots for baubles and glitter.

- Decorate the party room with balloons, baubles, tinsel, holly and laurel leaves. Edge the food table with tinsel.
- Dress up as Father Christmas, a Christmas fairy, or as a Christmas tree dressed in green with tinsel and baubles attached. Or go as a present dressed in red with ribbons.
- Traditional food and Christmas cake. Or a Christmas log from a Swiss roll covered in chocolate icing and dusted with icing sugar 'snow'.
- For going home presents, give out paper or material stockings filled with nuts and Christmas sweets and a little wrapped present.

Swimming Party

Depending on the guests' ages, a paddling pool may be sufficient. Or go to the local swimming pool. Strictly supervise the children at all times.

- Make invitations in the shape of a swimming pool, or a fish, asking guests to come in beach wear with their swimming gear.
- Play water polo with a ball, and races if you are using a swimming pool; who can throw the rubber ring the furthest, in the water or in the garden; bobbing for apples in a bowl of water.
- Picnic outside on beach towels. Make fish-shaped biscuits and serve ice cream. A loaf tin cake decorated as a swimming pool or cut into a fish shape with wafer fins.

Firework Party

- Cut out firework-shaped invitations.
- Set up a barbecue so that you can eat outdoors.
- Serve baked potatoes, sausages, and hamburgers, toffee apples and popcorn.
- Help children to toast marshmallows and chestnuts on long forks or skewers.
- Have plenty of helpers to organize and supervise the firework display.
- Give each child a sparkler so they can draw patterns or write their name in the air.
- The cake could be made in the shape of a rocket by standing Swiss rolls on end and covering them in icing. Use wafers for wings and an ice cream cone for the nose.

It's a Knockout

Divide guests into two differently coloured teams, or 'spotty' and 'stripey' teams.

- Colour invitations to match - state which team the children are a member of so they come appropriately dressed.
- Hold three-legged races, wheelbarrow races, welly throwing and relay obstacle races. Give teams prizes. Have lots of games so each team wins some.
- Serve picnic tea with differently coloured cakes for each team.
- Give out appropriately coloured 'sporty' going home presents.